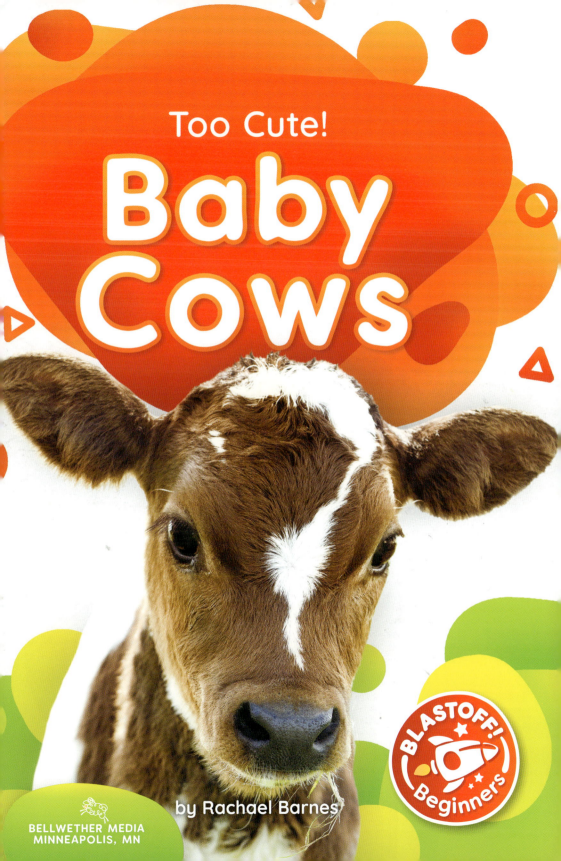

Blastoff! Beginners are developed by literacy experts and educators to meet the needs of early readers. These engaging informational texts support young children as they begin reading about their world. Through simple language and high frequency words paired with crisp, colorful photos, Blastoff! Beginners launch young readers into the universe of independent reading.

Sight Words in This Book

a	eat	is	she	this
and	from	look	some	to
are	have	make	soon	will
at	help	on	the	
big	her	play	them	
down	in	run	they	

This edition first published in 2023 by Bellwether Media, Inc.

No part of this publication may be reproduced in whole or in part without written permission of the publisher. For information regarding permission, write to Bellwether Media, Inc., Attention: Permissions Department, 6012 Blue Circle Drive, Minnetonka, MN 55343.

Library of Congress Cataloging-in-Publication Data

Names: Barnes, Rachael, author.
Title: Baby cows / by Rachael Barnes.
Description: Minneapolis, MN : Bellwether Media, 2023. | Series: Blastoff! beginners: Too cute! | Includes bibliographical references and index. | Audience: Ages 4-7 | Audience: Grades K-1
Identifiers: LCCN 2022012967 (print) | LCCN 2022012968 (ebook) | ISBN 9781644876695 (library binding) | ISBN 9781648347153 (ebook)
Subjects: LCSH: Calves--Juvenile literature. | Cows--Juvenile literature.
Classification: LCC SF205 .B37 2023 (print) | LCC SF205 (ebook) | DDC 636.2/07--dc23/eng/20220330
LC record available at https://lccn.loc.gov/2022012967
LC ebook record available at https://lccn.loc.gov/2022012968

Text copyright © 2023 by Bellwether Media, Inc. BLASTOFF! BEGINNERS and associated logos are trademarks and/or registered trademarks of Bellwether Media, Inc.

Editor: Christina Leaf   Designer: Jeffrey Kollock

Printed in the United States of America, North Mankato, MN.

Table of Contents

A Baby Cow!	4
Life as a Calf	6
All Grown Up!	20
Baby Cow Facts	22
Glossary	23
To Learn More	24
Index	24

A Baby Cow!

Look at the baby cow. Hello, calf!

Life as a Calf

Calves are born on farms. They are big babies!

Mom licks her calf clean. This helps them **bond**.

Young calves drink milk from mom's **udder**.

udder

Some calves drink milk from a **bottle**.

Calves lie down to rest.
Straw makes a soft bed!

straw

Calves play!
They run
and kick.

Calves begin to eat grass outside. They eat hay in barns.

hay

All Grown Up!

This **heifer** is grown. Soon she will have her own calf!

Baby Cow Facts

Cow Life Stages

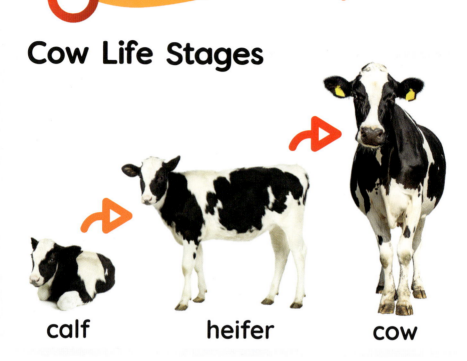

calf   heifer   cow

A Day in the Life

drink mom's milk   lie down to rest   play

Glossary

bond — to become close

bottle — an object that holds things to drink

heifer — a young female cow that has not had a baby

udder — the body part of a female cow that gives milk

To Learn More

ON THE WEB

FACTSURFER

Factsurfer.com gives you a safe, fun way to find more information.

1. Go to www.factsurfer.com.

2. Enter "baby cows" into the search box and click 🔍.

3. Select your book cover to see a list of related content.

Index

barns, 18
bed, 14
big, 6
bond, 8
born, 6
bottle, 12, 13
clean, 8
cow, 4
drink, 10, 12

eat, 18
farms, 6
grass, 18, 19
hay, 18
heifer, 20, 21
helps, 8
kick, 16
licks, 8
lie, 14

milk, 10, 12
mom, 8, 10
play, 16
rest, 14
run, 16
straw, 14, 15
udder, 10

The images in this book are reproduced through the courtesy of: Mihail Fedorenko, front cover; Eric Isselee, pp. 3, 4, 5, 22 (calf, heifer); Eva Lorenz, pp. 6-7; Andrea J Smith, pp. 8-9; smereka, p. 10; Irina Kononova, pp. 10-11; tum3123, pp. 12-13; Tarica, pp. 14-15; Beatrics Foord-St-Laurent, p. 16; imageBROKER/ Alamy, pp. 16-17; Olekshiichik, p. 18; Clara Bastian, pp. 18-19, 22 (cow), 23 (heifer); dropStock, pp. 20-21; ABB Photo, p. 22 (drink milk); VidEst, p. 22 (rest); Brenda Koehne, p. 22 (play); Ben Schonewille, p. 23 (bond); Caftor, p. 23 (bottle); Photobank.kiev.ua, p. 23 (udder).